Francis Frith's

DERBYSHIRE
LIVING MEMORIES

photographs of the mid twentieth century

Francis Frith's

DERBYSHIRE
LIVING MEMORIES

Roly Smith

First published in the United Kingdom in 2001 by
Frith Book Company Ltd

Hardback Edition 2001
ISBN 1-85937-330-5

Paperback Edition 2003
ISBN 1-85937-686-x

British Library Cataloguing in Publication Data

Francis Frith's Derbyshire Living Memories
Roly Smith

Frith Book Company Ltd
Frith's Barn, Teffont,
Salisbury, Wiltshire SP3 5QP
Tel: +44 (0) 1722 716 376
Email: info@francisfrith.co.uk
www.francisfrith.co.uk

Front Cover: **LONG EATON,** *Market Place c1950* L198002

Frontispiece: **CHESTERFIELD,** *Knifesmithgate c1955* C83014

*The colour-tinting is for illustrative purposes only,
and is not intended to be historically accurate*

Printed and bound in Great Britain

contents

Francis Frith: Victorian Pioneer   7

Frith's Archive - A Unique Legacy   10

Derbyshire Living Memories – An Introduction   12

South-East Derbyshire   18

North-East Derbyshire   41

The White Peak   59

The Dark Peak   95

Index   115

Free Mounted Print Voucher   119

Francis Frith: Victorian Pioneer

FRANCIS FRITH, Victorian founder of the world-famous photographic archive, was a complex and multi-talented man. A devout Quaker and a highly successful Victorian businessman, he was both philosophic by nature and pioneering in outlook.

By 1855 Francis Frith had already established a wholesale grocery business in Liverpool, and sold it for the astonishing sum of £200,000, which is the equivalent today of over £15,000,000. Now a very rich man, he was able to indulge his passion for travel. As a child he had pored over travel books written by early explorers, and his fancy and imagination had been stirred by family holidays to the sublime mountain regions of Wales and Scotland. 'What lands of spirit-stirring and enriching scenes and places!' he had written. He was to return to these scenes of grandeur in later years to 'recapture the thousands of vivid and tender memories', but with a different purpose. Now in his thirties, and captivated by the new science of photography, Frith set out on a series of pioneering journeys to the Nile regions that occupied him from 1856 until 1860.

Intrigue and Adventure

He took with him on his travels a specially-designed wicker carriage that acted as both dark-room and sleeping chamber. These far-flung journeys were packed with intrigue and adventure. In his life story, written when he was sixty-three, Frith tells of being held captive by bandits, and of fighting 'an awful midnight battle to the very point of surrender with a deadly pack of hungry, wild dogs'. Sporting flowing Arab costume, Frith arrived at Akaba by camel seventy years before Lawrence, where he encountered 'desert princes and rival sheikhs, blazing with jewel-hilted swords'.

During these extraordinary adventures he was assiduously exploring the desert regions bordering the Nile and patiently recording the antiquities and peoples with his camera. He was the first photographer to venture beyond the sixth cataract. Africa was still the mysterious 'Dark Continent', and Stanley and Livingstone's historic meeting was a decade into the future. The conditions for picture taking confound belief. He laboured for hours in his wicker dark-room in the sweltering heat of the desert, while the volatile chemicals fizzed dangerously in their trays. Often he was forced to work in remote tombs and caves where conditions were cooler. Back in London he exhibited his photographs and was 'rapturously cheered' by members of the Royal Society. His reputation as a photographer was made overnight. An eminent modern historian has likened their impact on the population of the time to that on our own generation of the first photographs taken on the surface of the moon.

Venture of a Life-Time

Characteristically, Frith quickly spotted the opportunity to create a new business as a specialist publisher of photographs. He lived in an era of immense and sometimes violent change. For the poor in the early part of Victoria's reign work was a drudge and the hours long, and people had precious little free time to enjoy themselves. Most had no transport other than a cart or gig at their disposal, and had not travelled far beyond the

boundaries of their own town or village. However, by the 1870s, the railways had threaded their way across the country, and Bank Holidays and half-day Saturdays had been made obligatory by Act of Parliament. All of a sudden the ordinary working man and his family were able to enjoy days out and see a little more of the world.

With characteristic business acumen, Francis Frith foresaw that these new tourists would enjoy having souvenirs to commemorate their days out. In 1860 he married Mary Ann Rosling and set out with the intention of photographing every city, town and village in Britain. For the next thirty years he travelled the country by train and by pony and trap, producing fine photographs of seaside resorts and beauty spots that were keenly bought by millions of Victorians. These prints were painstakingly pasted into family albums and pored over during the dark nights of winter, rekindling precious memories of summer excursions.

The Rise of Frith & Co

Frith's studio was soon supplying retail shops all over the country. To meet the demand he gathered about him a small team of photographers, and published the work of independent artist-photographers of the calibre of Roger Fenton and Francis Bedford. In order to gain some understanding of the scale of Frith's business one only has to look at the catalogue issued by Frith & Co in 1886: it runs to some 670 pages, listing not only many thousands of views of the British Isles but also many photographs of most European countries,

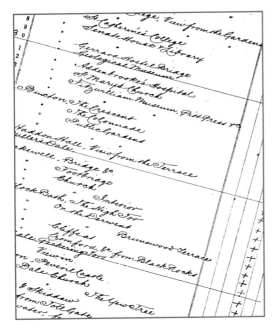

and China, Japan, the USA and Canada – note the sample page shown above from the hand-written *Frith & Co* ledgers detailing pictures taken. By 1890 Frith had created the greatest specialist photographic publishing company in the world, with over 2,000 outlets – more than the combined number that Boots and W H Smith have today! The picture on the right shows the *Frith & Co* display board at Ingleton in the Yorkshire Dales (left of window). Beautifully constructed with a mahogany frame and gilt inserts, it could display up to a dozen local scenes.

Postcard Bonanza

The ever-popular holiday postcard we know today took many years to develop. In 1870 the Post Office issued the first plain cards, with a pre-printed stamp on one face. In 1894 they allowed other publishers' cards to be sent through the mail with an attached adhesive halfpenny stamp. Demand grew rapidly, and in 1895 a new size of postcard was permitted called the court card, but there was little room for illustration. In 1899, a year after Frith's death, a new card measuring 5.5 x 3.5 inches became the standard format, but it was not until 1902 that the divided back came into being, with address and message on one face and a full-size illustration on the other. *Frith & Co* were in the vanguard of postcard development, and Frith's sons Eustace and Cyril continued their father's monumental task, expanding the number of views offered to the public and recording more and more places in Britain, as the coasts and countryside were opened up to mass travel.

Francis Frith died in 1898 at his villa in Cannes, his great project still growing. The archive he created continued in business for another seventy years. By 1970 it contained over a third of a million pictures of 7,000 cities, towns and villages. The massive photographic record Frith has left to us stands as a living monument to a special and very remarkable man.

Frith's Archive: A Unique Legacy

FRANCIS FRITH'S legacy to us today is of immense significance and value, for the magnificent archive of evocative photographs he created provides a unique record of change in 7,000 cities, towns and villages throughout Britain over a century and more. Frith and his fellow studio photographers revisited locations many times down the years to update their views, compiling for us an enthralling and colourful pageant of British life and character.

We tend to think of Frith's sepia views of Britain as nostalgic, for most of us use them to conjure up memories of places in our own lives with which we have family associations. It often makes us forget that to Francis Frith they were records of daily life as it was actually being lived in the cities, towns and villages of his day. The Victorian age was one of great and often bewildering change for ordinary people, and though the pictures evoke an impression of slower times, life was as busy and hectic as it is today.

We are fortunate that Frith was a photographer of the people, dedicated to recording the minutiae of everyday life. For it is this sheer wealth of visual data, the painstaking chronicle of changes in dress, transport, street layouts, buildings, housing, engineering and landscape that captivates us so much today. His remarkable images offer us a powerful link with the past and with the lives of our ancestors.

Today's Technology

Computers have now made it possible for Frith's many thousands of images to be accessed almost instantly. In the Frith archive today, each photograph is carefully 'digitised' then stored on a CD Rom. Frith archivists can locate a single photograph amongst thousands within seconds. Views can be catalogued and sorted under a variety of categories of place and content to the immediate benefit of researchers.

Inexpensive reference prints can be created for them at the touch of a mouse button, and a wide range of books and other printed materials assembled and published for a wider, more general readership. The day-to-day workings of the archive are very different from how they were in Francis Frith's time: imagine the herculean task of sorting through eleven tons of glass negatives as Frith had to do to locate a particular sequence of pictures! Yet the archive still prides itself on maintaining the same high

See Frith at www.francisfrith.co.uk

standards of excellence laid down by Francis Frith, including the painstaking cataloguing and indexing of every view.

It is curious to reflect on how the internet now allows researchers in America and elsewhere greater instant access to the archive than Frith himself ever enjoyed. Many thousands of individual views can be called up on screen within seconds on one of the Frith internet sites, enabling people living continents away to revisit the streets of their ancestral home town, or view places in Britain where they have enjoyed holidays. Many overseas researchers welcome the chance to view special theme selections, such as transport, sports, costume and ancient monuments.

We are certain that Francis Frith would have heartily approved of these modern developments in imaging techniques, for he himself was always working at the very limits of Victorian photographic technology.

The Value of the Archive Today

Because of the benefits brought by the computer, Frith's images are increasingly studied by social historians, by researchers into genealogy and ancestry, by architects, town planners, and by teachers and schoolchildren involved in local history projects.

In addition, the archive offers every one of us an opportunity to examine the places where we and our families have lived and worked down the years. Highly successful in Frith's own era, the archive is now, a century and more on, entering a new phase of popularity.

The Past in Tune with the Future

Historians consider the Francis Frith Collection to be of prime national importance. It is the only archive of its kind remaining in private ownership and has been valued at a million pounds. However, this figure is now rapidly increasing as digital technology enables more and more people around the world to enjoy its benefits.

Francis Frith's archive is now housed in an historic timber barn in the beautiful village of Teffont in Wiltshire. Its founder would not recognize the archive office as it is today. In place of the many thousands of dusty boxes containing glass plate negatives and an all-pervading odour of photographic chemicals, there are now ranks of computer screens. He would be amazed to watch his images travelling round the world at unimaginable speeds through network and internet lines.

The archive's future is both bright and exciting. Francis Frith, with his unshakeable belief in making photographs available to the greatest number of people, would undoubtedly approve of what is being done today with his lifetime's work. His photographs, depicting our shared past, are now bringing pleasure and enlightenment to millions around the world a century and more after his death.

Derbyshire Living Memories
An Introduction

At the crossroads of Britain

Derbyshire stands on the border between highland and lowland Britain, and therefore can be said to enjoy the best of both worlds. The scenic contrasts of the county range from the rugged Pennine moorlands of the Dark Peak, to the pastoral lowland meadows of the Lower Dove and Trent.

This position at the crossroads of Britain is reflected in the effect that Man has had on the landscape. Towns and villages in the Peak District are often small and isolated and built not of the red brick of the lowlands, but of the native stone. There are also many more stone-built reminders of the ancient past, including the many burial mounds or 'lows' which crown so many hills in the Peak District, and surviving prehistoric monuments such as the Arbor Low stone circle, near Parsley Hay.

Once you have crossed the north-south border, north of Ashbourne, the hedgerows and arable fields which typify the Midlands give way to mile after mile of drystone walls criss-crossing stony pastures, where pastoral farming of sheep and cattle predominates.

The rocks beneath

In terms of geology, Derbyshire is divided into four distinct regions, which in turn have shaped its landscape and towns and villages. These are: the southern clay and sandstone area, roughly south of a line from Derby to Ashbourne; the sandy coal measures east of Derby and Chesterfield with the band of magnesian limestone around Bolsover and Whitwell; the central limestone plateau of the White Peak between Ashbourne and Castleton; and the high millstone grit moorlands in the north of the county, which are usually known as the Dark Peak.

The largely Carboniferous rocks of the northern half of the county were laid down in semi-tropical conditions around 350 million years ago, when what was to become Derbyshire was several degrees south of the Equator and flooded by a warm, shallow sea. This was when the enormously thick beds of limestone, which are now exposed as the White Peak plateau, were laid down as millions of tiny sea creatures died and drifted down to the sea bed. Following a series of minor volcanic events, the limestone was covered by beds of coarse grit and silt deposited by rivers flowing from the north. This was compressed and compacted to form the alternating layers of millstone grit and softer shales which now form the moorland areas known as the Dark Peak and the broad shale valleys below, now occupied by Derbyshire's major rivers such as the Derwent and Wye.

The whole 'sandwich' was overlaid yet again by the coal-bearing tropical rain forests of the Carboniferous period, which created the coal measures of the former Derbyshire-Nottinghamshire coalfield, running from Chesterfield south to Ilkeston.

At the end of the Carboniferous period, these sedimentary rocks were subjected to very strong folding and faulting, followed by an uplift in the earth's crust which created the famous Derbyshire Dome anticline. The action of glaciers and the frost-thaw conditions of successive Ice Ages wore down the dome from the centre, creating the now familiar up-turned horseshoe of gritstone and shale with the coal measures on either side, and the older limestone exposed in the middle.

The red-coloured sandstones and clays of the south of the county were laid down after the Carboniferous rocks to the north in the arid, semi-desert conditions of the Triassic period, up to 280 million years ago. These rocks are much softer and more susceptible to erosion. They create the richer and more

fertile soils of the south, over which has been deposited the alluvium deposits of the Trent, Dove and Derwent.

Not surprisingly, the varied geology of the county has played a major part in the building materials and styles of the vernacular architecture of its towns and villages.

Man's influence

The first evidence of Man in Derbyshire is found on the bleak, inhospitable moors of the Dark Peak. Tiny slivers of flint - known as microliths - have been found in the sides of the groughs or haggs which dissect the moorland. These slivers had been hafted onto arrows which were discarded by Mesolithic (Middle Stone Age) hunters, perhaps 10,000 years ago.

Few remains of the temporary camps of these first hunter-gatherers have survived, but most of the great prehistoric monuments of Derbyshire are to be found in the uplands of the Peak District. Chief among these is the isolated prostrate stone circle and henge at Arbor Low, high on the White Peak plateau near Parsley Hay, which is sometimes dubbed 'the Stonehenge of the North'.

There are estimated to be at least 500 barrows - burial mounds - scattered across the county, mostly dating from the Bronze Age. Nearly all are situated on hilltops or high points in the landscape and, paradoxically most have the suffix 'low' from the Old English 'hlaw' for a burial mound or hill. The Iron Age (about 2,000 years ago) was the age of the hillfort, and impressive examples can be found at places like Mam Tor at the head of the Hope Valley and Fin Cop, overlooking Monsal Dale.

It was the abundant and easily accessible lead ore found in the limestone areas of the White Peak which first attracted the Romans into Derbyshire, in the latter part of the 1st century. Forts were built at Navio, near Brough in the Hope Valley, and at Melandra, near Glossop at the entrance to Longdendale. Later, more substantial settlements were made around the warm springs at Buxton (Aquae Arnemetia) and on the outskirts of modern Derby, where the fort of Little Chester (Derventio) has been excavated.

The period between the Romans and the Normans - usually termed 'the Dark Ages' - saw a wonderful flowering of art and sculpture, witnessed by Derbyshire's outstanding collection of Saxon preaching crosses. Excellent examples can be found at Bakewell, Bradbourne, Eyam, Hope and Ilam in the Peak District, while Repton's surviving Saxon crypt and chancel bear evidence to this sleepy little town's former importance as a famous Mercian monastery and the burial place of the Saxon St Wystan.

The first Anglian people who colonised the Peak District were known as the Pecsaete, or people of the Peak, while the south of the county fell under the influence of the powerful kingdom of Middle England - Mercia. For a period, Derbyshire appears to have acted as a buffer between the states of Mercia and Northumbria before Mercia finally attained ascendancy by the end of the 8th century. It was during this time that Derby first got its name from the Old Scandinavian tongue, meaning the 'place where deer are seen', later going back to its Saxon name of 'Northworthy' and then reverting to the Danish "Derby" in the 10th century.

By the time of the Norman Conquest, much of the present-day pattern of villages and towns in Derbyshire was well-established, as is illustrated by the Domesday Book of 1086. Only seven churches - at Ashbourne, Bakewell, Bradbourne, Darley, Hope, Repton and Wirksworth - are mentioned as being in existence before the Conquest, and some still show signs of Saxon work today, particularly those at Bradbourne and Repton.

Much of the Derbyshire part of the Peak District was held by the king at the time of Domesday, and was part of the Royal Forest of the Peak - a 40-square-mile hunting ground preserved for royalty. The Forest was administered, along with the lead mines, from Peveril Castle at Castleton. This was built by William Peveril, who was one of the Conquerer's illegitimate sons. He also built the original stronghold at Haddon Hall, near Bakewell. Later Norman castles and fortified manors were built at Codnor, South Wingfield, Hardwick, and Haddon, and there are a fine Norman churches at Melbourne, Steetley, and Ault Hucknall, and traces of Norman work in the churches at Bakewell and Barlborough, among many others.

During the Middle Ages, the wealth of Derbyshire was founded on its lead and wool.

Some of the fine churches, such as the beautiful, Perpendicular-towered 'Cathedral of the Peak' at Tideswell, and All Saints at Youlgreave, are founded upon those riches.

The Middle Ages also saw the growth of the large estates. The great Derbyshire families grew rich on them and their produce, building the county's wonderful heritage of stately homes and parklands: the Cavendishes, Dukes of Devonshire, at Bolsover, Chatsworth, and Hardwick; the Vernons, Dukes of Rutland, at Haddon and Sudbury; the Stanhopes at Elvaston; the Harpur-Crewes at Calke, and the Curzons at Kedleston.

This was also the time of the first enclosures of the large medieval open fields, from the moorland which still covered much of the upland part of the county. These large, irregular fields on the outskirts of villages contrast strongly with the narrow linear fields leading from the village crofts which were the villager's own strip fields. The pattern of medieval enclosure is well shown in White Peak villages such as Chelmorton, Monyash and Wardlow, where it has been 'fossilised' by the drystone walls.

The linear bumps and hollows on the limestone plateau are evidence of the work of 't'owd man' - the local name for former generations of lead miners. Lead mining was

an important industry in the White Peak for well over 1,000 years, starting with the Romans and ending in the 19th century when cheaper imports became available. There are estimated to be about 30,000 abandoned workings in the area, the best preserved of which is the Magpie Mine, near Sheldon, which was worked more or less continuously for 200 years. Peak District lead miners were also usually farmers as well, and this dual economy existed in the area as the mainstay of the local economy for centuries, bequeathing a rich legacy in the language and landscape.

It was the power of the Derbyshire rivers - particularly the Derwent - which attracted the first real industrialists to the county. Foremost among these were John Lombe and George Sorocold, who established Derby's Silk Mill in 1718, and Richard Arkwright, who built the first successful water-powered cotton mill at Cromford in 1771, the first 'model village' for his workers nearby, and other cotton mills at Cressbrook, Bakewell and elsewhere. Cromford was where Arkwright first pioneered the ideas of mass production and could well be described as one of the birthplaces of the Industrial Revolution. Downstream, Jedediah Strutt's cotton mill at Belper was founded a few years later in 1776. He later developed a calico and tape mill in Derby.

The presence of relatively easily obtainable supplies of coal, from the North Derbyshire, Leicestershire and South Derbyshire, and Yorkshire, Nottinghamshire and Derbyshire coalfields, all on the east of the county, made Derbyshire one of the biggest sources of power in the late 19th and early 20th centuries. By 1910 there were estimated to be over 175 coal mines in Derbyshire, employing 52,000 people. Output was more than 16.5 million tons in 1906, and the proximity of ironstone and limestone placed the county in an ideal position for iron and steel production.

The building of the Derby Canal by Benjamin Outram in 1796 proved to be a key element in turning a prosperous market town into a leading centre of industry.

The famous Derby porcelain factory had been established by William Duesbury around 1750, and, helped by local supplies of coal, an iron-founding industry followed. The same Benjamin Outram had, with Francis Beresford, founded the famous Butterley Iron Works in 1790. He was also a joint promoter (with Richard Arkwright) of the Cromford Canal, designed to link Arkwright's mills at Cromford to the River Trent and the Midlands.

Railways followed, including George Stephenson's Derby to Leeds line through the Derwent Valley. By 1840 no less than three

railway companies were operating lines to Derby, to and from Nottingham, Leeds and Birmingham respectively. Within five years they had amalgamated to form the Midland Railway. Benefitting from its central position on the east coast line, Derby became a major railway centre and terminus. The Midland Railway established its locomotive and carriage works there soon after its formation, and more foundries soon followed in the town to provide other components for the burgeoning railways. The construction of the Midland Line, providing the lucrative link between London and Manchester through the Wye Valley and the hills of the Peak District, followed in 1863.

Industrial towns like Derby and Chesterfield expanded rapidly during the 19th century, and by the time it was awarded city status a hundred years later in 1977, Derby had become one of the major industrial and engineering centres of the Midlands.

In the smaller towns and villages of Derbyshire, a distinctive vernacular architecture had developed, usually based on the underlying geology of the area. Thus in the limestone area of the White Peak, cottages are built of limestone rubble, usually with more regular gritstone quoins and window surrounds. Like the warm, brown gritstone town houses of the larger villages, like Bakewell and Matlock, these older houses are often roofed in gritstone slabs, which have sometimes later been replaced by blue Welsh slate. Out in the country, the barns and farm buildings also reflect the available building stone, which is repeated in the endless miles of drystone walls of the Peak and in the

hawthorn hedgerows of the stoneless south and east. In the former coalfield towns and villages of the east of the county, and in the clay vales to the south of Ashbourne, Midland red brick is the most common building material. In the larger industrial towns served by railways, such as Derby, Chesterfield, Belper and Ilkeston, blue engineering bricks are often employed on larger industrial buildings where Victorian civic pride is reflected in grandiose town halls.

Derbyshire today is perhaps best known for the Peak District National Park, the first to be designated in Britain in 1951 in recognition of its outstanding scenery. It covers 555 square miles of the north of the county, taking in the limestone plateau and dales of the White Peak, and the brooding gritstone moors and edges of the Dark Peak. Over 22 million days of visits are made to the National Park every year, making it the second-most visited National Park in the world.

But those visitors who only flock to the hills and dales of the Peak are missing a lot of what Derbyshire has to offer. It is indeed a county of contrasts, and the south and east of the county also have a rich heritage of stately homes, wide parklands, spacious views and charming towns and villages, illustrated here by Francis Frith's photographs.

This book is divided into four sections, starting with the towns and villages of south east Derbyshire, centred on Derby, Alfreton and Ikeston; then moving to the coalfield belt to the north and east; and then, moving into the Peak District. The pretty limestone villages of the White Peak are visited first, followed by the gritstone settlements of the Dark Peak.

South-East Derbyshire

Alfreton
Watchorn Memorial Park c1960 A199011
This manicured avenue of trees, in the former coal mining town
of Alfreton, has grown considerably in the 40 years since this
photograph was taken. But the park still provides a welcome haven
of peace for residents near the centre of town.

Ambergate, The Village c1955 A203022
In the mid-50s when this photograph was taken, the main A6 trunk road, which passes through the centre of Ambergate, looked like a quiet country byway. Ambergate stands where the River Amber joins the mighty Derwent, which is crossed by a fine bridge. The background is provided by Ambergate's lovely Shining Cliff Woods.

Belper, Long Row c1955 B437016
The terraced houses and cobbled street of Long Row at Belper is one of the many legacies left by Jedediah Strutt who, with Richard Arkwright, brought industry to the town in the late 18th century. The houses on the right of the street date from about this time, and were provided by Strutt for his workers at the nearby cotton mills, powered by the River Derwent.

**Belper
High Pavement
c1955** B437018
High Pavement is one of many Belper streets which run steeply down to the River Derwent, with the green hills of this part of south Derbyshire forming the background. The white doorway of the Nag's Head pub stands on the right of the picture, with the chimney of one of the town's many mills just visible to its left.

◄ **Bretby**
Bretby Park c1955
B768002
Bretby Park, seen here on its hilltop site across the lake in the 600-acre park, was built between 1812-13 by Sir Jeffrey Wyatville in a castellated, mock-Gothic style. It replaced the Earl of Chesterfield's 17th-century building, designed by Inigo Jones, which was demolished in the 18th century. The building is now a hospital.

◄ Belper
King Street 1951
B437020
King Street is one of Belper's main shopping streets. It runs east off the A6 Bridge Street, near the station, and up the hill towards the Market Place, which can be seen in the background. Note the impressive array of awnings which shade the shopfronts, and bank buildings and Boots the Chemist on the right.

▼ Church Gresley
The Maurice Lea Memorial
Park c1955 C402003
This 1950s view shows the wonderfully ornate bandstand which stands at the centre of the well-kept Maurice Lea Memorial Park in the former coal-mining village of Church Gresley. The village takes it name from the Gresley family who lived at nearby Drakelowe Hall, now best-known for its power stations.

◄ Derby
The Municipal Buildings
and Riverside Gardens
c1955 D24014
This view shows the imposing red-brick Municipal Buildings and rose-filled Riverside Gardens in the centre of Derby, as they looked in the mid-50s. Derby's industrial foundation is witnessed by the forest of chimneys of the textile mills on the River Derwent in the right background.

Duffield, King Street c1955 D159026
A slightly incongruous mock-Tudor thatched villa (centre) stands out among the gritstone cottages on either side in this 50s view of King Street, Duffield. Duffield is one of the finest small towns in Derbyshire, particularly noted for its fine range of Georgian houses in Town Street.

Duffield, The Bridge c1950 D159033
Motorists speeding through Duffield on the A6 miss this view of the fine buttressed bridge across the River Ecclesbourne. Duffield was an important place in medieval times, and the A6 passes by the foot of the tree-covered Castle Mound, the motte of what was once one of the most formidable Norman castles in England.

Findern, The Green c1965 F127003
It is a quiet summer's day on the Green at Findern, a small village three miles south-west of Derby. The white painted building in the centre of the photograph is the village Post Office, which is being visited by a local farmer who has parked his Land Rover outside. Findern is famous for the legend of a white narcissus, said to have been brought back from the Crusades by Sir Geoffrey de Fynderne, lord of the manor.

Heanor, The Memorial and Church c1960 H331123
The cenotaph-like War Memorial occupies the left foreground of this view of Heanor's park, while on the right, a group of three 60s youths eye the cameraman suspiciously. In the background, the stately Perpendicular tower of Heanor's Parish Church of St Lawrence dominates the view. The church was extensively rebuilt in 1868.

**Ilkeston
Town Centre c1965**
137064
Ilkeston is a busy
market town situated
high above the valley of
the River Erewash. This
60s view shows the
usual range of shops,
from Boots the Chemist
to F W Woolworths
and Wigfalls on the
right. Ilkeston is a
typical south
Derbyshire former
mining town, centred
on its fine medieval
parish church.

◄ **Long Eaton
Market Place c1950**
L198002
This is the Market Place
at Long Eaton, as it
looked in 1950.
Although still firmly in
Derbyshire, Long Eaton
has almost been
swallowed up by the
suburbs of nearby
Nottingham, across the
River Trent to the east.
The Empire Cinema
dominates to the right of
the picture, next door to
the arched entrance to
the Telford Library.

◀ **Ilkeston**
Bath Street c1965
I37070
The Borough Arms stands on the corner of Ilkeston's Market Place and Bath Street with East Street leading off to the right. We are looking down Bath Street in this mid-60s view of the town with shoppers filling the pavements with their prams and shopping bags.

▼ **Mapleton**
General View c1950
M348014
The village of Mapleton stands on the River Dove south of Ashbourne. The elegant arch of its bridge, the border with Staffordshire, can be seen in the centre of this general view of the village, taken around 1950. The field in the foreground shows the unmistakeable corrugations of the ridge and furrow of medieval cultivation.

◀ **Mapleton**
The Village c1950 M348027
An ornate metal sign bearing the coat of arms of the local lord of the manor distinguishes the Okeover Arms in the village of Mapleton, which also sold teas and ices when this photograph was taken in the 50s.

Milford, The Bridge c1955 M354005
This sweeping curve on the A6 leads from the handsome bridge which crosses the River Derwent at Milford, near Belper. In the distance can be seen the parish church of the Holy Trinity, built in 1848 in the Early English style by Moffat, a partner of Sir George Gilbert Scott. The terraced cottages of some of Jedediah Strutt's mill workers can be seen on the skyline.

New Sawley, The Marina c1955 N127012
Sawley Bridge Marina, on the Sawley Cut of the River Trent, south of Long Eaton, was already starting to cater for the ever-increasing boating trade when this photograph was taken in the mid-50s. In the background can be seen the cooling towers and chimneys of the Ratcliffe-on-Soar power stations.

Pentrich, The Church c1960 P236003
Pentrich, famous for its abortive 'Revolution' in 1817 of disenchanted stocking-makers, has now regained its peace. This view shows the battlemented hilltop parish church of St Matthew, which dates from the late 12th century and has a squat, Norman-looking tower.

Repton, Church End c1955 R298009
Thatched and half-timbered cottages - a rarity in Derbyshire - at Church End, Repton, as they looked in the mid-50s. This part of south Derbyshire did not have the abundant stone for its buildings which the north of the county enjoyed, so many villages have a definitely Midlands, rather than northern, feel about them.

Repton, The Old Mitre c1955 R298013
The many-gabled block of the Old Mitre Inn overlooks Repton's stepped and ball-topped Market Cross, which is claimed to be the spot where St Wystan first preached Christianity in the Midlands. Repton is now most famous for its public school, founded in 1556.

Repton
Repton School, The Arch c1955 R298033
This fine medieval arch marks the entrance to Repton's famous
public school, founded by Sir John Port of Etwall. It is by the
side of the former Saxon church of St Wystan (behind the
trees to the left) and was obviously once associated with it. In
the background can just be seen the mock-Tudor Pears
Memorial Hall, built in memory of the headmaster who
successfully put the school on the map between 1854-74.

Ripley, Sandham Lane c1955 R299006
Sandham Lane, Ripley, was an unmade road leading to Sandham Farm when this photograph was taken in the mid-50s. Now this once-quiet country lane is largely built up and lies to the south of the town founded on mining and Benjamin Outram's Butterley Iron Works.

South Normanton, Market Place c1955 S725004
How many people remember the embossed gold signs for 'Turog' brown bread, like that seen on the right of this photograph. Photographs like this remind us of a time when traffic was not a problem, and you could park outside the shop you were visiting. Those were the days!

South Normanton
Market Street c1955 S725010

Another view of South Normanton Market Street, showing a Ford Anglia van parked outside the Pinxton Co-operative Society's Furnishing Department store. A young boy hitches up his short trousers on the left, watched by grandad, and across the road, the White Lion stands opposite the Devonshire Arms, a very common pub name in these parts.

South Normanton
The Old Windmill c1955 S725012

Almost every English village once had its windmill, but by 1955, when this photograph was taken, most had gone, and South Normanton's former post mill was down to a skeletal framework, standing forlornly in a grassy meadow. Nothing remains today.

**Swadlincote
High Street c1955**
S454008
The south Derbyshire town of Swadlincote - usually abbreviated locally to 'Swad' - is another which was founded on the once-important coal mining industry. Today, of course, the mines are all closed, and Swadlincote, like many other Derbyshire towns, has had to reinvent itself. This 1950s view of the High Street shows it at the height of its economic prosperity.

Swanwick, Derby Road c1955 S724007
Swanwick, a small village halfway between Ripley and Alfreton and now bypassed by the A38 trunk road, has a parish church with a fine, pinnacled tower, seen in the centre of this 1950s photograph in Derby Road. To the left of the church is the Steam Packet public house, selling the local Shipstone's ales.

Swanwick, Derby Road c1955 S724016
Another view of Derby Road, Swanwick, a little further north, opposite Willgoose's newsagents shop, on the left. The billboards outside proclaim "Boom Week" in the 'Daily Mail' and that cricket news is important in the 'News Chronicle'. Local news, however, is provided by the 'Nottingham Post'.

Whatstandwell, The Station c1955 W347020
A footbridge over the Cromford Canal in the foreground leads from the village of Whatstandwell to the other bridge. This crosses the Midland line, which in turn leads to the station. The village, on the A6 between Belper and Matlock, gets its long and unusual name from a 14th-century landlord, Walter or "Wat" Stonewell.

Willington, The Village c1950 W557001
Willington has been at the hub of communications for two centuries. Standing close to the River Trent and the Trent and Mersey Canal south of Derby, and on the line of the Midland Railway, it is now near the under and overpasses of the junction between the A38 and A50. This 50s view shows the centre of the village in more tranquil times.

Willington, Oaks Lane c1955 W557003
The post-war building expansion is well shown in this mid-50s view of Oaks Lane, Willington. Semi-detached houses like these would have been snapped up by house-buyers wanting to be in commuting distance from Derby, just six miles away on the A38.

North-East Derbyshire

Barlborough
The Main Drive c1955 B803006
In this view through the main entrance door, the fine avenue of limes and topiary hedges lead up to Barlborough Hall, one of Derbyshire's finest Elizabethan mansions. Built in 1584 for Lord Justice Francis Rodes, it is thought to have been designed by Robert Smythson. It is now a private Roman Catholic school.

◄ **Barlborough Park Street c1955**
B803024

This is the view in the opposite direction from picture B803023, looking past the Market Cross down Park Street, towards the gated entrance to Barlborough Hall in the distance. The building on the right is interesting, built of sandstone with an elegant ground floor Georgian Venetian-style window.

◄ Barlborough High Street c1955

B803023

The ancient Market Cross with its sundial dominates the High Street in Barlborough, opposite the Rose and Crown public house, which is on the right of this 50s photograph. Note the pantiled roof of the house next door to the pub, and horse-drawn cart in the distance. In the background is Barlborough's distinctively-shaped water tower, known locally as 'the Egg Cup', it has been long since demolished.

▼ Barlborough High Street c1955

B803025

The same Venetian-windowed house as in photograph B803024 can be seen in the right distance. This view is from Eckington Road, looking towards the Market Cross. Note the superb red pantiled roof of the barn on the left, and the ornate mosaic memorial arch in front of it, built in the 19th century by William Hatfield de Rhodes in memory of his wife.

◄ Bolsover The Castle c1955

B133027

Bolsover Castle stands proudly on its limestone bluff in this view from the Chesterfield Road to the west. The first castle at Bolsover was built by William Peverel, the illegitimate son of William the Conqueror, but the present building dates mainly from Sir Charles Cavendish's romantic rebuilding of 1613-16, including the keep now known as the 'Little Castle'.

Bolsover, Market Place c1955 B133038
'Bolsover Illuminations', presumably of the castle, were being advertised on a banner
across the street in this view of the Market Place. Other shop signs visible are the
Nottingham Trustee Savings Bank; a branch of the well-known Chesterfield department
store, Eyres; and Wycherleys the chemists, the white-painted shop in the centre.

Brimington, High Street c1965 B603001
It is a quiet day in Brimington High Street in the 60s. On the right is the Methodist Church, which was celebrating its anniversary, next door is the local branch of the Chesterfield Co-operative Society, and in the distance can be seen the pinnacled tower of the parish church.

Brimington, Ringwood Road and Church c1965 B603002
The east end of Brimington's 19th-century parish church is just visible behind the trees in this view of the centre of the village, between Chesterfield and Staveley. The name of Ringwood Road refers to the early 19th-century mansion of Ringwood House, home of the Markham family, which stands to the north east.

Chesterfield, Market Place c1955 C83002
The red-brick clock tower of Chesterfield's Market Hall, built in 1857, dominates this 50s view. The covered market stalls fill the square below, as they still do today. Note the large poster on the tower advertising the National Savings scheme, popular in the immediate post-war years.

Chesterfield, High Street c1960 C83038
Two helmeted local 'bobbies' stride towards the camera in another view of the Market Place in Chesterfield, looking up the High Street towards the famous Crooked Spire of the parish church of St Mary and All Saints. In the centre of the photograph, the brewer's dray of P O Middleton makes a delivery to a local pub.

Chesterfield Knifesmithgate c1955 C83014
Here we are looking down Knifesmithgate, one of Chesterfield's oldest streets towards the distinctive spire of the parish church. It was named after the medieval cutlers who once traded here. The black and white, mock-Tudor half-timbered shops were mainly built between the wars.

Chesterfield, Holywell Street c1955 C83041
Prominent in this view of Holywell Street is the Odeon Cinema, Theatre and Ballroom, then showing Peter Sellers in 'The Battle of the Sexes'. The Odeon is now the Winding Wheel Theatre - named in tribute to the town's coal mining tradition - which has a fine reputation for travelling variety and popular music shows.

Clowne, The Dam c1950 C403003
The Dam is still the popular name for Clowne's reservoir at Harlesthorpe, north of the former coal-mining village. Clowne takes its unusual name from the old name of the River Poulter which runs through the village. To the east is Markland Grips, an Iron Age hillfort on an outcrop above a craggy limestone valley.

Clowne, The Cross c1950 C403007
The ball-topped sandstone Market Cross stands on its stepped base in the centre of Clowne, a former coal-mining village between Barlborough and Bolsover. Note The Anchor public house on the left, and the advertisement for Andrews Liver Salts in the right background.

◀ **Dronfield Chesterfield Road c1965** D177012
Thankfully Dronfield, between Chesterfield and Sheffield, is now bypassed by the A61, but the Chesterfield Road has never returned to the peacefulness evident in this mid-60s photograph. In the background is the spire of the parish church.

◀ **Clowne**
Mill Street c1950
C403009
A trader wheels a handcart down Mill Street on the right of this photograph. The former half-timbered Bowden Arms, now gone, stands on the right, while opposite are G Cowell's hardware store and L H Robotham's shop. Bystanders eye the Frith's cameraman quizzically.

▼ **Dronfield**
Church Street c1965
D177037
Fine Georgian bay-fronted houses front Church Street, Dronfield, in this photograph taken around 1965. In a recent Boundaries Commission review it was proposed to merge Dronfield with Sheffield, but there was fierce local opposition to the idea, and it remains firmly where it has always been, in Derbyshire.

◀ **Dronfield**
High Street c1965
D177041
There are a number of fine houses in Dronfield's High Street, notably the early 18th-century Manor House, which now serves as council offices. The fine Perpendicular tower and spire of the parish church of St John the Baptist can be seen in the centre background.

◄ **Eckington
High Street c1955**
E226002
Here we are looking
down Eckington High
Street towards the
imposing, pedimented
Methodist Chapel.
Non-conformism was
strong in the mining
villages and towns of
north-east Derbyshire
and the chapel played
an important part in the
lives of the mining
communities.

◀ **Eckington
Market Street c1955**

E226011

Another former colliery village, Eckington is a long, sprawling village with Market Street and High Street, now partly pedestrianised, extending for over a mile. Short-trousered youths scamper outside Harris and Sons drapers' shop on the left of this photograph, taken in the mid-1950s.

▼ **Killamarsh
Rectory Road c1960**

K116021

New council estates, like this one in Rectory Road, Killamarsh, seven miles north of Bolsover on the border of South Yorkshire, sprung up like mushrooms in the 1950s and 60s. Often, they gave working class people, like the coal and steel workers of Killamarsh, their first homes.

◀ **New Whittington
High Street c1955**

N128003

The name of the pub in the distance, The Miner's Arms, is significant, for New Whittington lies in the heart of the north-east Derbyshire coalfield, but is now submerged into the northern suburbs of Chesterfield. This mid-50s photograph again shows a virtually traffic-free road.

Old Whittington, The Monument c1955 O129001
This is a distant view of the ancient heart of Old Whittington, showing the sandstone Monument which commemorates the 'Glorious Revolution' of 1688, which was hatched here in this sleepy Chesterfield suburb. In the centre of the picture is Revolution House, where the Duke of Devonshire plotted the return of William of Orange.

Old Whittington, The Monument and Revolution House c1955 O129009
A closer view of the thatched Revolution House, centre, which was originally a public house known as
The Cock and Pynot (a local name for the magpie). It was here that the Duke of Devonshire and other local
noblemen schemed the downfall of King James II. It is now a museum, and a modern Cock and Magpie pub
now stands nearby.

Shirebrook, Main Street c1955 S450003
Shirebrook is a small town on the border with Nottinghamshire which grew up with, and was dominated by, the
growth of the Shirebrook and Langwith collieries. Now they are closed, along with most other collieries in the
north-east Derbyshire coalfield, the town has reverted to the kind of calm seen in this mid-50s view of the Main
Street.

Shirebrook, The Vic Inn c1955 S450008
The substantial red brick structure of the Vic, or Victoria, Inn at Shirebrook, seen here around 1955, pays tribute to the once-healthy economy of the town, when coal was king and the miners had plenty to spend in public houses such as this.

Upper Langwith, The Church c1955 U38001
The simple little 13th-century parish church of the Holy Cross at Upper Langwith, east of Bolsover and close to the border of Nottinghamshire, may not have a tower, but it is nevertheless a gem of Perpendicular architecture. Note the pinnacled south porch and long lancet window, just visible at the west end.

The White Peak

Alport
Mill Bridge c1960 A333024
Alport stands at the confluence of the Lathkill and Bradford rivers, near Youlgreave.
The Mill Bridge is a graceful, 18th-century single-arched structure near to the site of the
former corn mill at the entrance to the village.

Ashbourne, St Oswald's Church c1950 A66042
The novelist George Eliot described St Oswald's at Ashbourne as "the finest mere parish church in England" and it is one of the most interesting in the Peak District. The soaring, 212-foot Perpendicular-style spire is still the most obvious landmark in the busy little market town at the entrance to Dovedale.

Ashbourne, The Memorial Gardens c1955 A66021
This is the bandstand in the well-kept Memorial Gardens at Ashbourne, as it looked in the mid-50s. Little has changed today, and the gardens still impart an air of tranquility for the residents of the town.

Ashford in the Water
Old Cottages c1955 A324002
In a scene which has hardly changed for a hundred years, a young girl and her sister push their toy pram past an ancient ivy-covered limestone cottage which is providing tea for visitors. This view shows a corner of the pretty village of Ashford-in-the-Water, near Bakewell.

**Ashford
In the Water
Top Pump c1955**
A324012
The Top Pump, at the junction with the road to Monsal Head, is the scene of one of Ashford's famous well dressings, held annually in early June. These floral celebrations of the gift of water are unique to the Peak District, and Ashford is one of the most important centres, 'dressing' no less than six wells every year.

◄ **Bakewell
The Bridge c1955**
B6006
Bakewell's five-arched
14th-century bridge
over the River Wye is
one of its greatest
glories. It is still carrying
traffic 600 years after it
was built. The riverside
path on the left has now
been metalled, and
houses have been built
to the left, but little else
has changed.

◄ Bakewell
The Square c1955

B6003
Apart from some 'Keep Left' signs on the War Memorial Island in front of the Georgian Rutland Arms Hotel (left), the centre of Bakewell has not changed since this photograph of Rutland Square was taken. The elegant spire of All Saints Church still dominates in the right background.

▼ Bakewell
Bridge Street c1955

B6009
This photograph was taken by the side of Bakewell Bridge on the roadway which ran down a disused ancient ford. We are looking back along Bridge Street, now a one-way system, into the bustling market town. It is the largest in the Peak District with a population of just under 4,000.

◄ Bakewell
The Riverside Walk
and River Wye c1955

B6027
This is the view from one of the parapets of Bakewell Bridge looking south, downstream along the River Wye. The island on the left is still there, occupied by ducks and geese, while the Riverside Walk on the right is now backed by housing erected under the Bakewell town centre redevelopment plan.

◄ **Bonsall**
The Clatterway c1950
B485005
The name of The Clatterway, in the former lead-mining village of Bonsall, is thought to derive from the noise made by horse-drawn waggons as they descended the steep hill towards the Via Gellia road.

Bakewell
The Old Original Pudding Shop c1965 B6100
Originally a chandler's shop, this late 17th-century building in Bridge Street, Bakewell, became the home in the late 19th century of the famous Bakewell pudding - incidentally, never known as a 'tart' in Bakewell. The original recipe was obtained from the cook at the nearby Rutland Arms, who created it as a result of a mistake around 1860.

Bonsall
The Cross c1955 B485013
The steeply-sloping Market Place in the centre of Bonsall is dominated by its 17th-century Market Cross, encircled by 13 gritstone steps. In the background is the King's Head public house, one of a number which slaked the thirsts of generations of the lead miners who formed the majority of the population of this sleepy little limestone village.

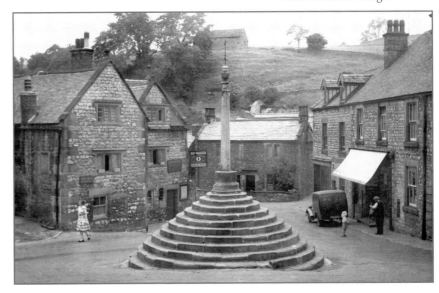

Bradwell
Church Street c1955
B486002
A lone cyclist pedals along Church Street in Bradwell. In the background is the parish church, built in 1868 but with some early-18th-century furnishings which were gifted by the Rev R B Somerset, a Fellow of Trinity College, Cambridge, and a native of this village on the edge of the Hope Valley.

Bradwell, St Ives c1955 B486015
This part of Bradwell, where the Bradwell Brook is crossed by a narrow bridge, is known as St Ives, presumably because of its resemblance to the tight streets of the Cornish village. Note the old-fashioned red telephone box just over the bridge, and the cottages spreading up the hillside behind.

Bradwell, The Village c1955 B486011
This is the view down Smithy Lane, Bradwell, looking towards the green escarpment of Bradwell Edge in the background. Note the non-conformist chapel on the extreme right. Most Peak District villages have such chapels, as non-conformism was common in mining communities like these.

Bradwell, Town Gate c1955 B486030
The steep hill in Bradwell known as Town Gate - 'gate' is an old Norse word meaning street - winds up past the white-painted White Hart public house on the right. The scene has not changed significantly in the last 50 years.

Castleton, Market Place c1955 C46045
The village war memorial (right), on the green in Castleton's Market Place, takes the form of a Celtic cross. In the background is Castleton Hall, a fine 17th-century building which is now the popular and always-busy Castleton Youth Hostel. Behind that are the distant shapes of Treak Cliff and Mam Tor.

**Castleton
The Village c1955**
C46072
The visitor window-shopping at the Blue John Craft Shop (est 1884) on the right of Castleton's Main Street, is well wrapped-up in his macintosh against the bitter Peak weather. The poster on his left advertises the 'Blue John Caverns', one of four show caves in this popular tourist honeypot.

**Castleton
Entrance to the
Speedwell Cavern
and Winnats Pass
c1950** C46056
The Speedwell Cavern,
on the left of this
photograph, is unique
among Derbyshire's
showcaves because the
visitor, having
descended 105 steps,
enters the cavern by
boat. The craggy
Winnats Pass in the
background is no longer
gated, but is still a
spectacular entrance to
Castleton from the
west.

◄ **Castleton**
Entrance to the Blue
John Cavern c1955
C46069
A walled, crater-like
depression in the side
of Treak Cliff forms the
entrance to the Blue
John Cavern, another of
Castleton's famous series
of showcaves in the
shadow of the 'Shivering
Mountain' of Mam Tor.
The Blue John was
another former lead
mine, famous for its
veins of the semi-
precious veined fluorspar
known as Blue John.

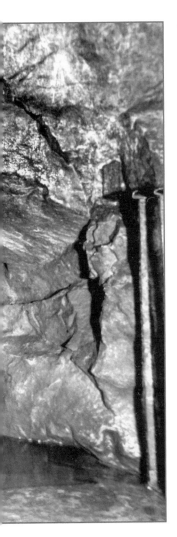

◄ **Castleton
Boat arriving
at the Bottomless Pit
Speedwell Cavern c1955**

C46067

The boat arrives at the landing place for the 'Bottomless Pit' in Castleton's Speedwell Cavern. The cavern was discovered by lead miners, who had cut the underground canal in an effort to drain their mine of excess water.

▼ **Chelmorton
The Village c1960**

C401009

Chelmorten is the highest village in Derbyshire, standing at well over 1,000 feet above the sea. In the centre of this 60s view of the entrance to the village is the unusual stone-built telephone box, next door to the old-fashioned traffic sign warning of the village school.

◄ **Crich
The Stand c1960**

C406003

Crich Stand is one of Derbyshire's most famous landmarks. Erected in 1922, this impressive inland lighthouse is a war memorial commemorating the local regiment, the Sherwood Foresters. The view extends over much of the White Peak and south across the rest of the county.

◀ **Edensor
The Village c1960**
E130006
The 6th Duke of Devonshire supervised the design of Edensor (pronounced "Ensor") in 1839 as a model estate village for his workers at nearby Chatsworth. The elegant spire of the parish church of St Peter was designed by Sir George Gilbert Scott and consecrated in 1867.

◀ **Cromford**
Willersley Castle
c1955 C193289
The original grandiose
pile of Willersley Castle,
near Cromford, was
built by Richard
Arkwright between
1782-88 as his mansion
near the village where
he first set up a
water-powered cotton
mill in 1771. He did not
live long enough to
enjoy it, because it
burnt down in 1791,
and he died before it
was rebuilt in its present
form.

▼ **Elton**
The Post Office and
Church c1950 E131013A
Elton is a typical White
Peak village, founded on
the dual economies of
farming and lead mining.
There are many fine
18th-century houses in the
village street, some of
which are seen in this
1950s photograph. The
pinnacled tower of the
parish church of All Saints,
reconstructed after its
steeple collapsed in 1812,
is seen on the left.

◀ **Great Hucklow**
The Village c1960
G180020
The former lead-mining
village of Great Hucklow
lies under the
escarpment of Hucklow
Edge, and was famous at
the time this photograph
was taken in the 1960s
for its outstanding
amateur dramatics
group led by Laurence
du Garde Peach and
known as the Hucklow
Players.

Great Hucklow, The Edge c1960 G180025
This view of Great Hucklow shows Hucklow Edge in the background, while to the left of the photograph can be seen some of the bumps and hollows left behind from the generations of lead mining which took place in and around the village.

Great Hucklow, World Gliding Championships 1954 G180035
The Derbyshire and Lancashire Gliding Club, based at Camphill, 1,360ft up on Hucklow Edge, had its finest moment when the World Gliding Championships, during which this photograph was taken, were held here in 1954. The club is still very active, operating from what must be one of the most scenic sites in the country.

Great Longstone, The Village c1955 G181004
This is the village green at Great Longstone, with the medieval village cross on the extreme right and the war memorial in the centre. Like many garage-less linear Peak District villages, Great Longstone is now cursed by parked cars, unlike when this photograph was taken. Then there were few cars to trouble pedestrians like the lady pushing her pram on the left.

Hartington, The Pond c1960 H330102
A family pose with their fine-looking pony by the village pond, or mere, at Hartington. The mere was an important place for many villages on the fast-draining White Peak plateau, and was one of the few places where stock could be led for drinking water.

▼ **Hartington, The Village c1955** H330106

This view shows the Market Square in Hartington, with the three-arched porch of the Town Hall, built in 1836, on the right. In the background is the Perpendicular-style tower of the parish church of St Giles, a mainly 13th- and 14th-century building. Today, the foreground of this view would be largely obscured by parked cars.

▼ **Hope, General View c1960** H113041

The then-popular breed of Shorthorn cattle dominate the foreground of this distant view of the village of Hope, which gave its name to the long east-west valley which ends at Castleton. The squat spire of Hope's 14th-century parish church of St Peter dominates the village, with the slopes of Win Hill in the background to the right.

▲ **Hope
The Village c1965**
H113057

Hope's two best-known hostelries, the Woodruffe Arms on the right and the Old Hall Hotel, centre, occupy either side of the main village street. The trees beyond the Woodruffe Arms are in the churchyard of St Peter's parish church.

◄ Dovedale
Ilam Hall c1965 D145066
Ilam Hall, now a National Trust property and youth hostel, was built in 1828 by the shipping magnate, Jesse Watts Russell, but was partly demolished in 1934. Watts Russell also converted the village of Ilam into an estate village in an extravagant, cottage ornee style, complete with mock Eleanor Cross in memory of his wife.

**Matlock
Hall Leys Pleasure
Gardens c1955**
M273025
The ornate, cast-iron
bandstand still occupies
the centreplace of
Matlock's Hall Leys
Pleasure Gardens,
although they are now
known simply as Hall
Leys Gardens. Matlock
is now the
administrative centre of
the county, with the
county council offices
occupying John
Smedley's former
hydro buildings.

▼ **Matlock, The Boating Lake c1955** M273031
Youngsters piloted by dad enjoy a trip on Matlock's boating lake in
the mid-50s. Matlock first came into prominence when John Smedley
founded his hydropathic establishment there in 1853. His fairy-tale
castle at Riber, which he designed himself in 1862, can be seen on
the hilltop to the right. It is now an unoccupied hollow shell.

▼ **Matlock Bath, The Heights of Abraham c1955** M47007
Visitors gather by the petrifying well outside the Pavilion - now the
Peak District Mining Museum - at Matlock Bath. In the background on
the skyline among the trees is the Prospect Tower at the summit of the
Heights of Abraham, now the terminus of a cable car ride.

▲ **Matlock Bath
The Heights of
Abraham c1955**
M47025
Another view of the main
road (the A6) through
Matlock Bath. The
wooded Heights of
Abraham, named after
their apparent
resemblance to the scene
of General Wolfe's
famous victory against
the French at Quebec in
1759, form the
backdrop. Note
Hodgkinson's Hotel and
the Spa Café on the left
of the picture and the
Amusement Arcade, now
demolished, on the right.

◄ **Matlock Bath
The Royal Cumberland
Cavern c1955** M47042
The Royal Cumberland
Cavern was one of several
show caves open to the
public in Matlock Bath in
the 1950s. No longer open,
it was well known for its
calcite formations and
traces of the old lead miners
who originally discovered it.
Here a guide explains what
appears to be a massive
roof fall in the cavern.

◀ **Middleton
Main Street 1951**
M122001
Middleton - full name
Middleton-by-Wirksworth -
was a quarrying and mining
village which produced the
famous Hopton Wood
stone. The narrow and
winding Main Street seen
here is typical of most
White Peak villages, and is
definitely not built for
modern traffic.

◀ Matlock Bath
Jubilee Bridge c1955

M47065
The Jubilee Bridge across the River Derwent at Matlock Bath is seen here fitted out for the Matlock Illuminations it was erected in honour of Queen Victoria's jubilee. Beneath the bridge, boaters enjoy a peaceful scull on the river.

▼ Middleton
The Village c1955 M122100

Newslade's Corner Shop on the entrance to Middleton was run by Mr and Mrs Thomas when this photograph was taken. General stores such as this were the nucleus of the village, a place where residents not only got most of their provisions before the days of town supermarkets, but also caught up on all the latest gossip about their neighbours.

◀ Miller's Dale
The Youth Hostel c1960

M79018
Miller's Dale Youth Hostel, overlooking the beautiful dale of the same name, occupies a stately Victorian mansion and has catered for thousands of young people since it first opened its doors. Among them was the botanist and broadcaster Dr David Bellamy, who claims to have learnt his talent for remembering the Latin names of plants while on a stay here.

Monsal Dale, General View c1955 M221012
This view from Monsal Head looks north-west up Upper Dale, with the huge embankment formed by the construction of the Midland Railway on the left. The River Wye winds peacefully through the valley beneath.

Monsal Dale, The Viaduct c1955 M221005
The famous view of the Monsal Dale Viaduct from Monsal Head, with the vast bulk of Fin Cop behind, has not changed since this photograph was taken in the mid-50s. The only difference is that steam trains, like that seen in the picture, no longer run on the Midland line. It has now been converted to the Monsal Trail, although there are long-term plans to re-open the line.

Monsal Dale, The Monsal Head Hotel c1955 M221016
The Monsal Head Hotel, seen here in the mid-50s, commands a spectacular view down into Monsal and Upper Dale from its slightly incongruous Tyrolean balcony which was added to the substantial limestone frontage many years ago.

Over Haddon
Lathkill Dale c1960 O77001
The series of weirs downstream from Over Haddon in Lathkill Dale were constructed to encourage trout to breed and spawn in this famous fishing river, which was famously described by Izaak Walton as "the purest and most transparent stream I ever yet saw, either at home or abroad".

Rowsley
The Peacock Hotel c1955
R300010
A distant view of the 17th-century Peacock Hotel at Rowsley. The Peacock takes its name from the coat of arms of the Manners family of nearby Bakewell, and is a favourite haunt of anglers who fish on the Derwent and Wye, which meet near the village.

Tideswell, Queen Street c1950 T46001
A largely traffic-free view of Queen Street, Tideswell in the 1950s. The village war memorial is prominent in the centre of the photograph, while the pinnacled tower of the parish church of St John the Baptist - 'the cathedral of the Peak' - can just be seen peeping over the rooftops.

Tideswell, Market Square c1950 T46005
Roses twine around the doorway of the cottage on the right in this 50s photograph of Tideswell's Market Square, with the Belle Vue Hotel (now gone) in the centre background. Like so many other White Peak villages, Tideswell was founded on the dual wealth won from farming and lead mining.

Two Dales, Red House c1955 T206014
The mock-Tudor gabled Red House at Two Dales, near Matlock, is now the home of a successful riding school and stables, where carriages and coaches can be hired for drives through the neighbouring villages and parklands of Chatsworth.

Winster, The Market House c1955 W569001
The 17th-century Old Market House at Winster was the first property to be acquired, in 1906, in the Peak District by the National Trust. The sandstone and brick structure originally had open archways on the ground floor, like that of the similar building in the centre of Bakewell.

Winster, Main Street c1955 W569002
Winster is one of the most perfectly-preserved 18th-century villages in the Peak District, as this 1950s view shows. Most of the cottages seen here date from that period, when Winster was a prosperous lead mining and farming centre.

Youlgreave, Church Street c1955 Y14001
The splendid Perpendicular tower of All Saints, Youlgreave, is one of the finest in the Peak District, and commands this view down Church Street. Note the charming Kate Greenaway-type silhouette sign above the village Post Office on the left, which uses the locally-preferred spelling of the village name - 'Youlgrave'.

Youlgreave, The Old Coach Road c1955 Y14009
Below the village of Youlgreave lies craggy Bradford Dale, through which runs the Old Coach Road, shown in this photograph. The cliffs on the right are known as Rhienstor, perhaps after the German river. The bridge on the left leads to the neighbouring village of Alport.

The Dark Peak

Bamford
The Marquis of Granby Hotel c1965 B483010
The imposing Marquis of Granby public house is a
landmark on the main Hope Valley road, near the turn to
Bamford and Derwent. Named after a prominent local
landlord, the pub sits beneath the long ridge of Shatton
Edge, seen here in the background.

Bamford, The Green c1965 B483023
The village green in the heart of the village of Bamford never was much of a green - just a few trees round the war memorial. The u-shaped stone on the extreme left is a distinctive Derbyshire 'squeezer' stile, designed to let people, but not stock through.

Baslow, Nether End c1955 B484004
The eastern end of the village of Baslow is known as Nether End. This 50s view is from outside the Cavendish Arms Hotel, looking west. Note the old-fashioned 'beacon of learning' school sign and AA logo near the sign advertising the hotel, which takes its name from the ruling Dukes of Devonshire from nearby Chatsworth.

Baslow
The Village c1955 B484006
This is a general view of the centre of Baslow as it looked in the
mid-50s, and which is hardly changed today. To the left is Coates'
grocery and druggist store, and on the extreme right, behind the old
Ford Popular car, is the gabled lych gate entrance to the churchyard
of the parish church of St Anne.

**Buxton
The Thermal Baths
c1955** B263006
The Thermal Baths
were built in 1854 by
Henry Currey and now
form the Cavendish
Shopping Arcade. In
the background can be
seen the imposing
façade of the Palace
Hotel. To the extreme
right, in sunshine, is the
Old Hall Hotel,
Buxton's oldest inn.
This is on the site of the
place where Mary
Queen of Scots stayed
when she visited the
town in the late 16th
century.

▼ **Buxton**
The Pavilion c1955 B263007

The ornate, cast-iron dome of Buxton's Pavilion was built in 1871 by the 7th Duke of Devonshire, as he invested much of the money he gained from his mineral interests in the Peak District towards expanding the spa town. In the background to the left is the tower of the Georgian parish church of St John the Baptist.

▼ **Buxton**
The Crescent c1955 B263008

Perhaps Buxton's greatest architectural glory is John Carr's elegant, sweeping curve of The Crescent, built in 1784 by the 5th Duke of Devonshire as he tried to make Buxton a rival to Bath. Designed as a hotel, it has recently been restored by English Heritage and others after years of neglect, but it still seeks a new use.

▲ **Buxton**
Peter Watson
Camping Grounds
by the Dane c1960
B263301

The Peak District has always been a popular place for weekend camping trips for the teeming populations of the nearby towns and cities of the industrial north. This is one such site by the River Dane to the west of Buxton, as it looked in the 1960s. Note the then popular bell tents, and the sleeping bags hung out to air.

◄ **Buxworth**
Brierley Green c1955
B790304
The gritstone village of
Buxworth is east of Whaley
Bridge, below the slopes of
Chinley Churn, and on the
main railway line between
Buxton and Stockport. This
50s photograph shows the
elevated section of the line
on the right, as it passes
above that part of the
village known as Brierley
Green.

Buxworth, New Road c1955 B790305
A typical gritstone terrace of cottages on New Road, with cycles left leaning outside one of them, right centre. New Road leads by the side of the River Goyt towards Furniss Vale and New Mills, to the north.

Calver, The Village c1950 C399045
This crossroads west of the village of Calver is known as Calver Sough - a sough (pronounced "suff") being a drainage tunnel designed to take water out of lead mines. There are traffic lights here today, at the busy junction of the Bakewell-Grindleford and Baslow-Stoney Middleton roads, and the petrol station on the right of the picture is no longer there.

Calver, Cliff College c1950 C399013
Cliff College, just outside the village of Calver under Curbar Edge, is a Methodist Teacher Training College which is also used for conferences and other events. In this photograph the façade was covered in a vigorous growth of ivy, which has since been removed.

Chapel-en-le-Frith, View from the Station c1940 C400008
The name of the Peak District town of Chapel-en-le-Frith means literally 'the chapel in the forest'. It was originally the site of a chapel in the medieval Royal Forest of the Peak, where kings and princes hunted deer, wolf and wild boar. This 1940s view from the station, which is some way south of the town, shows just how many trees were still left then.

**Chapel-en-le-Frith
The Stocks c1960**
C400032
The ancient stocks in
Chapel's Market Square
probably date from the
Cromwellian period,
and have recently been
renovated. They were
designed to take two
offenders at a time, as
shown by the holes for
their arms and legs, as
they endured the
humiliation of
becoming the targets for
the rotten vegetables
thrown by bystanders at
the nearby weekly
market.

Chapel-en-le-Frith, Market Street c1940 C400011
Market Street is devoid of traffic in this 1940s picture, looking east towards the town centre. Although known as Market Street, the weekly market at Chapel is held in the cobbled Market Square, which stands above the main thoroughfare.

Chapel-en-le-Frith, The Ferodo Research Laboratories c1960 C400039
Still the biggest single employer in Chapel, Ferodo was founded by local man Herbert Froode (of which 'Ferodo' is an anagram) who first developed a brake block for horse-drawn carts and later successfully developed it for cars, lorries and buses. In this 1960s photograph, Ferodo's Research Laboratories had just been opened.

Combs
The view cross the Combs c1950 C404005
The hamlet of Combs lies to the south-west of Chapel-en-le-Frith,
sheltering in the hollow formed by the escarpment known as Combs
Edge. Note the spotted and horned Shorthorn cattle in the
foreground, in the 1950s the most popular dairy breed in the Peak
District but now replaced by the ubiquitous black and white Friesians.

◄ **Grindleford
The Village Square
c1960** G182031
Grindleford does not
really have a village
square, as this
photograph suggests.
The war memorial on
the right, on the road to
Hathersage, is based on
the design of Eyam's
Saxon cross, while the
Methodist Church on
the left was built in
1905 and replaced an
earlier building where
John Wesley preached
in 1776.

◄ Grindleford
The Village c1955

G182015

A view of the Main Road in Grindleford, a Derwentside village to the north of Bakewell. The Derwent is crossed by a fine bridge which is to the right of the bend in the road at the foot of the hill. The village stores on the right of the photograph is now an art gallery.

▼ Hathersage
The Village c1955   H38015

The George Hotel (centre) stands at the junction of the Main Street with the road to Grindleford, in the centre of the Hope Valley village of Hathersage. Next door was the Corner Cupboard Café in this 1950s picture, opposite the old 'flaming beacon' school road sign, on the extreme left.

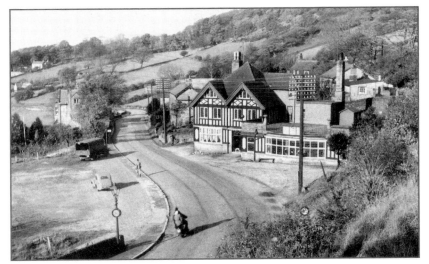

◄ Hathersage
The Millstone Inn c1955

H38001

Originally a simple, low vernacular building, the Millstone Inn had been converted to a garish, black and white gabled mock-Tudor structure by the time of this photograph. It is named after the millstones which were extensively quarried from the local 'edges' of gritstone. Note the motorcyclist with his pillion passenger as they lean into the corner approaching the village from Sheffield.

Hayfield
Market Street c1960
H298002
A couple of lads, one on his bike, chat outside the bank (right) on the corner of Market Street. Across the street, a group of younger children congregate outside the sweet shop, in a reminder of the days before heavy traffic made this kind of scene impossible.

◀ **Ladybower
The Reservoir c1955**
L294005
These are the impressive wrought iron entrance gates to the Ladybower Dam, above Bamford in the Upper Derwent Valley. The reservoir was opened in September, 1945 by King George VI and Queen Elizabeth, who unveiled a memorial tablet and opened the two overflow shafts, one of which is seen to the right of this photograph.

◄ Hayfield
from the Snake Path
c1960 H298042

This is a distant view of Hayfield in the valley of the River Sett, taken from the Snake Path, a famous right-of-way which leads across a shoulder of Kinder Scout, the highest point of the Peak District. This was opened by the Hayfield and Kinder Scout Ancient Footpaths Association in 1897. For many years, it was the only right-of-way to cross Kinder.

▼ New Mills
The Grammar School
c1960 N126011

The Grammar School at New Mills, seen here in the centre distance of this general view across the town, is an ancient foundation. For many years it took children from as far away as the Hope Valley for their secondary education. Behind the school is the Gothic spire of St George's church and the rolling foothills of the Peak District.

◄ New Mills
Market Street c1965
N126030

The modern façade of the New Mills Co-operative Society, on the right of this 60s picture, looks a little out of place in New Mills's Market Street. The 'new mills' which gave the town its name were the cotton mills powered by the Rivers Goyt and Sett, which meet in the town in the rocky gorge known as The Torrs.

Tintwistle
Old Road c1960 T204029
Tintwistle stands at the western entrance to the Longdendale and
the Woodhead Pass, a major cross-Pennine route for many
centuries. Locally pronounced "Tinsel", this busy little community
is mainly made up of typical gritstone terraces, like those seen in
this photograph of Old Road.

Index

Alfreton 18
Alport 59
Ambergate 19
Ashbourne 60
Ashford in the Water 61, 62-63
Bakewell 64-65, 66-67
Bamford 95, 96
Barlborough 41, 42-43
Baslow 96-97
Belper 19, 20-21, 22-23
Bolsover 43, 44-45
Bonsall 66, 67
Bradwell 67, 68, 69
Bretby 22
Brimington 46
Buxton 98-99, 100-101
Buxworth 101, 102
Calver 102, 103
Castleton 69, 70-71, 72-73, 74-75
Chapel-en-le-Frith 103, 104-105, 106
Chelmorton 75
Chesterfield 47, 48-49, 50
Church Gresley 23

Clowne 50, 51, 52-53
Combs 107
Crich 75
Cromford 76-77
Derby 23
Dovedale 81
Dronfield 52, 53
Duffield 24
Eckington 54-55
Edensor 76
Elton 77
Findern 25
Great Hucklow 77, 78
Great Longstone 79
Grindleford 108-109
Hartlington 79, 80
Hathersage 109
Hayfield 110-111, 112
Heanor 25
Hope 80-81
Ilkeston 26-27, 28-29
Killamarsh 55
Ladybower 112
Long Eaton 28
Mapleton 29
Matlock 82-83, 84

Matlock Bath 84-85, 86-87
Middleton 86, 87
Milford 30
Millers' Dale 87
Monsale 88, 89
New Mills 113
New Sawley 30
New Whittington 55
Old Whittington 56, 57
Over Haddon 90
Pentrich 31
Repton 31, 32, 33
Ripley 34
Rowsley 90
Shirebrook 57, 58
South Normanton 34, 35
Swandlincote 36-37
Swanwick 38
Tideswell 91
Tintwistle 114
Two Dales 92
Upper Langwith 58
Whatslandwell 39
Willington 40
Winster 92, 93
Youlgreave 93, 94

Frith Book Co Titles

www.francisfrith.co.uk

The Frith Book Company publishes over 100 new titles each year. A selection of those currently available is listed below. For latest catalogue please contact Frith Book Co.
Town Books 96 pages, approximately 100 photos. **County and Themed Books** 128 pages, approximately 150 photos (unless specified). All titles hardback with laminated case and jacket, except those indicated pb (paperback)

Amersham, Chesham & Rickmansworth (pb)	1-85937-340-2	£9.99
Andover (pb)	1-85937-292-9	£9.99
Aylesbury (pb)	1-85937-227-9	£9.99
Barnstaple (pb)	1-85937-300-3	£9.99
Basildon Living Memories (pb)	1-85937-515-4	£9.99
Bath (pb)	1-85937-419-0	£9.99
Bedford (pb)	1-85937-205-8	£9.99
Bedfordshire Living Memories	1-85937-513-8	£14.99
Belfast (pb)	1-85937-303-8	£9.99
Berkshire (pb)	1-85937-191-4	£9.99
Berkshire Churches	1-85937-170-1	£17.99
Berkshire Living Memories	1-85937-332-1	£14.99
Black Country	1-85937-497-2	£12.99
Blackpool (pb)	1-85937-393-3	£9.99
Bognor Regis (pb)	1-85937-431-x	£9.99
Bournemouth (pb)	1-85937-545-6	£9.99
Bradford (pb)	1-85937-204-x	£9.99
Bridgend (pb)	1-85937-386-0	£7.99
Bridgwater (pb)	1-85937-305-4	£9.99
Bridport (pb)	1-85937-327-5	£9.99
Brighton (pb)	1-85937-192-2	£8.99
Bristol (pb)	1-85937-264-3	£9.99
British Life A Century Ago (pb)	1-85937-213-9	£9.99
Buckinghamshire (pb)	1-85937-200-7	£9.99
Camberley (pb)	1-85937-222-8	£9.99
Cambridge (pb)	1-85937-422-0	£9.99
Cambridgeshire (pb)	1-85937-420-4	£9.99
Cambridgeshire Villages	1-85937-523-5	£14.99
Canals And Waterways (pb)	1-85937-291-0	£9.99
Canterbury Cathedral (pb)	1-85937-179-5	£9.99
Cardiff (pb)	1-85937-093-4	£9.99
Carmarthenshire (pb)	1-85937-604-5	£9.99
Chelmsford (pb)	1-85937-310-0	£9.99
Cheltenham (pb)	1-85937-095-0	£9.99
Cheshire (pb)	1-85937-271-6	£9.99
Chester (pb)	1-85937-382 8	£9.99
Chesterfield (pb)	1-85937-378-x	£9.99
Chichester (pb)	1-85937-228-7	£9.99
Churches of East Cornwall (pb)	1-85937-249-x	£9.99
Churches of Hampshire (pb)	1-85937-207-4	£9.99
Cinque Ports & Two Ancient Towns	1-85937-492-1	£14.99
Colchester (pb)	1-85937-188-4	£8.99
Cornwall (pb)	1-85937-229-5	£9.99
Cornwall Living Memories	1-85937-248-1	£14.99
Cotswolds (pb)	1-85937-230-9	£9.99
Cotswolds Living Memories	1-85937-255-4	£14.99
County Durham (pb)	1-85937-398-4	£9.99
Croydon Living Memories (pb)	1-85937-162-0	£9.99
Cumbria (pb)	1-85937-621-5	£9.99
Derby (pb)	1-85937-367-4	£9.99
Derbyshire (pb)	1-85937-196-5	£9.99
Derbyshire Living Memories	1-85937-330-5	£14.99

Devon (pb)	1-85937-297-x	£9.99
Devon Churches (pb)	1-85937-250-3	£9.99
Dorchester (pb)	1-85937-307-0	£9.99
Dorset (pb)	1-85937-269-4	£9.99
Dorset Coast (pb)	1-85937-299-6	£9.99
Dorset Living Memories (pb)	1-85937-584-7	£9.99
Down the Severn (pb)	1-85937-560-x	£9.99
Down The Thames (pb)	1-85937-278-3	£9.99
Down the Trent	1-85937-311-9	£14.99
East Anglia (pb)	1-85937-265-1	£9.99
East Grinstead (pb)	1-85937-138-8	£9.99
East London	1-85937-080-2	£14.99
East Sussex (pb)	1-85937-606-1	£9.99
Eastbourne (pb)	1-85937-399-2	£9.99
Edinburgh (pb)	1-85937-193-0	£8.99
England In The 1880s	1-85937-331-3	£17.99
Essex - Second Selection	1-85937-456-5	£14.99
Essex (pb)	1-85937-270-8	£9.99
Essex Coast	1-85937-342-9	£14.99
Essex Living Memories	1-85937-490-5	£14.99
Exeter	1-85937-539-1	£9.99
Exmoor (pb)	1-85937-608-8	£9.99
Falmouth (pb)	1-85937-594-4	£9.99
Folkestone (pb)	1-85937-124-8	£9.99
Frome (pb)	1-85937-317-8	£9.99
Glamorgan	1-85937-488-3	£14.99
Glasgow (pb)	1-85937-190-6	£9.99
Glastonbury (pb)	1-85937-338-0	£7.99
Gloucester (pb)	1-85937-232-5	£9.99
Gloucestershire (pb)	1-85937-561-8	£9.99
Great Yarmouth (pb)	1-85937-426-3	£9.99
Greater Manchester (pb)	1-85937-266-x	£9.99
Guildford (pb)	1-85937-410-7	£9.99
Hampshire (pb)	1-85937-279-1	£9.99
Harrogate (pb)	1-85937-423-9	£9.99
Hastings and Bexhill (pb)	1-85937-131-0	£9.99
Heart of Lancashire (pb)	1-85937-197-3	£9.99
Helston (pb)	1-85937-214-7	£9.99
Hereford (pb)	1-85937-175-2	£9.99
Herefordshire (pb)	1-85937-567-7	£9.99
Herefordshire Living Memories	1-85937-514-6	£14.99
Hertfordshire (pb)	1-85937-247-3	£9.99
Horsham (pb)	1-85937-432-8	£9.99
Humberside (pb)	1-85937-605-3	£9.99
Hythe, Romney Marsh, Ashford (pb)	1-85937-256-2	£9.99
Ipswich (pb)	1-85937-424-7	£9.99
Isle of Man (pb)	1-85937-268-6	£9.99
Isle of Wight (pb)	1-85937-429-8	£9.99
Isle of Wight Living Memories	1-85937-304-6	£14.99
Kent (pb)	1-85937-189-2	£9.99
Kent Living Memories(pb)	1-85937-401-8	£9.99
Kings Lynn (pb)	1-85937-334-8	£9.99

Available from your local bookshop or from the publisher

Frith Book Co Titles (continued)

Title	ISBN	Price	Title	ISBN	Price
Lake District (pb)	1-85937-275-9	£9.99	Sherborne (pb)	1-85937-301-1	£9.99
Lancashire Living Memories	1-85937-335-6	£14.99	Shrewsbury (pb)	1-85937-325-9	£9.99
Lancaster, Morecambe, Heysham (pb)	1-85937-233-3	£9.99	Shropshire (pb)	1-85937-326-7	£9.99
Leeds (pb)	1-85937-202-3	£9.99	Shropshire Living Memories	1-85937-643-6	£14.99
Leicester (pb)	1-85937-381-x	£9.99	Somerset	1-85937-153-1	£14.99
Leicestershire & Rutland Living Memories	1-85937-500-6	£12.99	South Devon Coast	1-85937-107-8	£14.99
Leicestershire (pb)	1-85937-185-x	£9.99	South Devon Living Memories (pb)	1-85937-609-6	£9.99
Lighthouses	1-85937-257-0	£9.99	South East London (pb)	1-85937-263-5	£9.99
Lincoln (pb)	1-85937-380-1	£9.99	South Somerset	1-85937-318-6	£14.99
Lincolnshire (pb)	1-85937-433-6	£9.99	South Wales	1-85937-519-7	£14.99
Liverpool and Merseyside (pb)	1-85937-234-1	£9.99	Southampton (pb)	1-85937-427-1	£9.99
London (pb)	1-85937-183-3	£9.99	Southend (pb)	1-85937-313-5	£9.99
London Living Memories	1-85937-454-9	£14.99	Southport (pb)	1-85937-425-5	£9.99
Ludlow (pb)	1-85937-176-0	£9.99	St Albans (pb)	1-85937-341-0	£9.99
Luton (pb)	1-85937-235-x	£9.99	St Ives (pb)	1-85937-415-8	£9.99
Maidenhead (pb)	1-85937-339-9	£9.99	Stafford Living Memories (pb)	1-85937-503-0	£9.99
Maidstone (pb)	1-85937-391-7	£9.99	Staffordshire (pb)	1-85937-308-9	£9.99
Manchester (pb)	1-85937-198-1	£9.99	Stourbridge (pb)	1-85937-530-8	£9.99
Marlborough (pb)	1-85937-336-4	£9.99	Stratford upon Avon (pb)	1-85937-388-7	£9.99
Middlesex	1-85937-158-2	£14.99	Suffolk (pb)	1-85937-221-x	£9.99
Monmouthshire	1-85937-532-4	£14.99	Suffolk Coast (pb)	1-85937-610-x	£9.99
New Forest (pb)	1-85937-390-9	£9.99	Surrey (pb)	1-85937-240-6	£9.99
Newark (pb)	1-85937-366-6	£9.99	Surrey Living Memories	1-85937-328-3	£14.99
Newport, Wales (pb)	1-85937-258-9	£9.99	Sussex (pb)	1-85937-184-1	£9.99
Newquay (pb)	1-85937-421-2	£9.99	Sutton (pb)	1-85937-337-2	£9.99
Norfolk (pb)	1-85937-195-7	£9.99	Swansea (pb)	1-85937-167-1	£9.99
Norfolk Broads	1-85937-486-7	£14.99	Taunton (pb)	1-85937-314-3	£9.99
Norfolk Living Memories (pb)	1-85937-402-6	£9.99	Tees Valley & Cleveland (pb)	1-85937-623-1	£9.99
North Buckinghamshire	1-85937-626-6	£14.99	Teignmouth (pb)	1-85937-370-4	£7.99
North Devon Living Memories	1-85937-261-9	£14.99	Thanet (pb)	1-85937-116-7	£9.99
North Hertfordshire	1-85937-547-2	£14.99	Tiverton (pb)	1-85937-178-7	£9.99
North London (pb)	1-85937-403-4	£9.99	Torbay (pb)	1-85937-597-9	£9.99
North Somerset	1-85937-302-x	£14.99	Truro (pb)	1-85937-598-7	£9.99
North Wales (pb)	1-85937-298-8	£9.99	Victorian & Edwardian Dorset	1-85937-254-6	£14.99
North Yorkshire (pb)	1-85937-236-8	£9.99	Victorian & Edwardian Kent (pb)	1-85937-624-X	£9.99
Northamptonshire Living Memories	1-85937-529-4	£14.99	Victorian & Edwardian Maritime Album (pb)	1-85937-622-3	£9.99
Northamptonshire	1-85937-150-7	£14.99	Victorian and Edwardian Sussex (pb)	1-85937-625-8	£9.99
Northumberland Tyne & Wear (pb)	1-85937-281-3	£9.99	Villages of Devon (pb)	1-85937-293-7	£9.99
Northumberland	1-85937-522-7	£14.99	Villages of Kent (pb)	1-85937-294-5	£9.99
Norwich (pb)	1-85937-194-9	£8.99	Villages of Sussex (pb)	1-85937-295-3	£9.99
Nottingham (pb)	1-85937-324-0	£9.99	Warrington (pb)	1-85937-507-3	£9.99
Nottinghamshire (pb)	1-85937-187-6	£9.99	Warwick (pb)	1-85937-518-9	£9.99
Oxford (pb)	1-85937-411-5	£9.99	Warwickshire (pb)	1-85937-203-1	£9.99
Oxfordshire (pb)	1-85937-430-1	£9.99	Welsh Castles (pb)	1-85937-322-4	£9.99
Oxfordshire Living Memories	1-85937-525-1	£14.99	West Midlands (pb)	1-85937-289-9	£9.99
Paignton (pb)	1-85937-374-7	£7.99	West Sussex (pb)	1-85937-607-x	£9.99
Peak District (pb)	1-85937-280-5	£9.99	West Yorkshire (pb)	1-85937-201-5	£9.99
Pembrokeshire	1-85937-262-7	£14.99	Weston Super Mare (pb)	1-85937-306-2	£9.99
Penzance (pb)	1-85937-595-2	£9.99	Weymouth (pb)	1-85937-209-0	£9.99
Peterborough (pb)	1-85937-219-8	£9.99	Wiltshire (pb)	1-85937-277-5	£9.99
Picturesque Harbours	1-85937-208-2	£14.99	Wiltshire Churches (pb)	1-85937-171-x	£9.99
Piers	1-85937-237-6	£17.99	Wiltshire Living Memories (pb)	1-85937-396-8	£9.99
Plymouth (pb)	1-85937-389-5	£9.99	Winchester (pb)	1-85937-428-x	£9.99
Poole & Sandbanks (pb)	1-85937-251-1	£9.99	Windsor (pb)	1-85937-333-x	£9.99
Preston (pb)	1-85937-212-0	£9.99	Wokingham & Bracknell (pb)	1-85937-329-1	£9.99
Reading (pb)	1-85937-238-4	£9.99	Woodbridge (pb)	1-85937-498-0	£9.99
Redhill to Reigate (pb)	1-85937-596-0	£9.99	Worcester (pb)	1-85937-165-5	£9.99
Ringwood (pb)	1-85937-384-4	£7.99	Worcestershire Living Memories	1-85937-489-1	£14.99
Romford (pb)	1-85937-319-4	£9.99	Worcestershire	1-85937-152-3	£14.99
Royal Tunbridge Wells (pb)	1-85937-504-9	£9.99	York (pb)	1-85937-199-x	£9.99
Salisbury (pb)	1-85937-239-2	£9.99	Yorkshire (pb)	1-85937-186-8	£9.99
Scarborough (pb)	1-85937-379-8	£9.99	Yorkshire Coastal Memories	1-85937-506-5	£14.99
Sevenoaks and Tonbridge (pb)	1-85937-392-5	£9.99	Yorkshire Dales	1-85937-502-2	£14.99
Sheffield & South Yorks (pb)	1-85937-267-8	£9.99	Yorkshire Living Memories (pb)	1-85937-397-6	£9.99

See Frith books on the internet at www.francisfrith.co.uk

FRITH PRODUCTS & SERVICES

Francis Frith would doubtless be pleased to know that the pioneering publishing venture he started in 1860 still continues today. A hundred and forty years later, The Francis Frith Collection continues in the same innovative tradition and is now one of the foremost publishers of vintage photographs in the world. Some of the current activities include:

Interior Decoration

Today Frith's photographs can be seen framed and as giant wall murals in thousands of pubs, restaurants, hotels, banks, retail stores and other public buildings throughout the country. In every case they enhance the unique local atmosphere of the places they depict and provide reminders of gentler days in an increasingly busy and frenetic world.

Product Promotions

Frith products are used by many major companies to promote the sales of their own products or to reinforce their own history and heritage. Frith promotions have been used by Hovis bread, Courage beers, Scots Porage Oats, Colman's mustard, Cadbury's foods, Mellow Birds coffee, Dunhill pipe tobacco, Guinness, and Bulmer's Cider.

Genealogy and Family History

As the interest in family history and roots grows world-wide, more and more people are turning to Frith's photographs of Great Britain for images of the towns, villages and streets where their ancestors lived; and, of course, photographs of the churches and chapels where their ancestors were christened, married and buried are an essential part of every genealogy tree and family album.

Frith Products

All Frith photographs are available Framed or just as Mounted Prints and Posters (size 23 x 16 inches). These may be ordered from the address below. From time to time other products - Address Books, Calendars, Table Mats, etc - are available.

The Internet

Already fifty thousand Frith photographs can be viewed and purchased on the internet through the Frith websites and a myriad of partner sites.

For more detailed information on Frith companies and products, look at these sites:

www.francisfrith.co.uk
www.francisfrith.com
(for North American visitors)

See the complete list of Frith Books at:

www.francisfrith.co.uk

This web site is regularly updated with the latest list of publications from the Frith Book Company. If you wish to buy books relating to another part of the country that your local bookshop does not stock, you may purchase on-line.

For further information, trade, or author enquiries please contact us at the address below:
The Francis Frith Collection, Frith's Barn, Teffont, Salisbury, Wiltshire, England SP3 5QP.
Tel: +44 (0)1722 716 376 Fax: +44 (0)1722 716 881 Email: sales@francisfrith.co.uk

See Frith books on the internet at www.francisfrith.co.uk

FREE MOUNTED PRINT

CHOOSE ANY IMAGE FROM THIS BOOK

Mounted Print
Overall size 14 x 11 inches

Fill in and cut out this voucher and return
it with your remittance for £2.25 (to cover postage and handling). Offer valid for delivery to UK addresses only.

Choose any photograph included in this book.
Your SEPIA print will be A4 in size. It will be mounted in a cream mount with a burgundy rule line (overall size 14 x 11 inches).

Order additional Mounted Prints at HALF PRICE (only £7.49 each*)
If you would like to order more Frith prints from this book, possibly as gifts for friends and family, you can buy them at half price (with no additional postage and handling costs).

Have your Mounted Prints framed
For an extra £14.95 per print* you can have your mounted print(s) framed in an elegant polished wood and gilt moulding, overall size 16 x 13 inches (no additional postage and handling required).

---

* IMPORTANT!

These special prices are only available if you order at the same time as you order your free mounted print. You must use the ORIGINAL VOUCHER on this page (no copies permitted). We can only despatch to one address.

Send completed Voucher form to:
The Francis Frith Collection, Frith's Barn, Teffont, Salisbury, Wiltshire SP3 5QP

Voucher **for FREE** *and Reduced Price Frith Prints*

Please do not photocopy this voucher. Only the original is valid, so please fill it in, cut it out and return it to us with your order.

Picture ref no	Page no	Qty	Mounted @ £7.49	Framed + £14.95	Total Cost
		1	Free of charge*	£	£
			£7.49	£	£
			£7.49	£	£
			£7.49	£	£
			£7.49	£	£
			£7.49	£	£
Please allow 28 days for delivery			* Post & handling (UK)	£2.25	
			Total Order Cost	£	

Title of this book . . . .

I enclose a cheque/postal order for £ . . . .
made payable to 'The Francis Frith Collection'

OR please debit my Mastercard / Visa / Switch / Amex card
(credit cards please on all overseas orders), details below

Card Number

Issue No (Switch only)   Valid from (Amex/Switch)

Expires   Signature

Name Mr/Mrs/Ms . . . .

Address . . . .

. . . .

. . . .

. . . . Postcode . . . .

Daytime Tel No . . . .

Email . . . .

Valid to 31/12/05

Would you like to find out more about Francis Frith?

We have recently recruited some entertaining speakers who are happy to visit local groups, clubs and societies to give an illustrated talk documenting Frith's travels and photographs. If you are a member of such a group and are interested in hosting a presentation, we would love to hear from you.

Our speakers bring with them a small selection of our local town and county books, together with sample prints. They are happy to take orders. A small proportion of the order value is donated to the group who have hosted the presentation. The talks are therefore an excellent way of fundraising for small groups and societies.

Can you help us with information about any of the Frith photographs in this book?

We are gradually compiling an historical record for each of the photographs in the Frith archive. It is always fascinating to find out the names of the people shown in the pictures, as well as insights into the shops, buildings and other features depicted.

If you recognize anyone in the photographs in this book, or if you have information not already included in the author's caption, do let us know. We would love to hear from you, and will try to publish it in future books or articles.

Our production team

Frith books are produced by a small dedicated team at offices in the converted Grade II listed 18th-century barn at Teffont near Salisbury, illustrated above. Most have worked with the Frith Collection for many years. All have in common one quality: they have a passion for the Frith Collection. The team is constantly expanding, but currently includes:

Jason Buck, John Buck, Douglas Mitchell-Burns, Ruth Butler, Heather Crisp, Isobel Hall, Julian Hight, Peter Horne, James Kinnear, Karen Kinnear, Tina Leary, David Marsh, Sue Molloy, Kate Rotondetto, Dean Scource, Eliza Sackett, Terence Sackett, Sandra Sampson, Adrian Sanders, Sandra Sanger, Julia Skinner, Lewis Taylor, Shelley Tolcher and Lorraine Tuck.